GW01459435

Eleanor Roosevelt:
An Extraordinary Life
of Activism and Influence

In the verdant beauty of the Hudson Valley, where the noble river meanders through New York's fertile landscapes, Eleanor Roosevelt, a remarkable woman of unmatched fortitude, first drew breath on a crisp autumn morning. Born on October 11, 1884, she entered a world that was both steeped in privilege and haunted by the weight of expectation. Little did the world know that this unassuming child would become an indomitable force, shaping the very fabric of American history.

Eleanor's lineage traced back to illustrious beginnings, with her ancestral roots reaching deep into the annals of American lore. She was the niece of President Theodore Roosevelt, a man of great energy and conviction. Yet, her own immediate family, while socially prominent, carried with it a deep sense of melancholy. Her father, Elliott Roosevelt, an alcoholic and a victim of mental instability, struggled to navigate the choppy waters of life. This family legacy of turmoil and tragedy would lay the groundwork for Eleanor's later commitment to empathy and compassion.

However, it was in the loving embrace of her mother, Anna Hall Roosevelt, that Eleanor found solace. Anna, known for her gentle nature and philanthropic endeavors, nurtured the budding spirit of her daughter.

From an early age, Eleanor was instilled with a profound sense of duty and an unyielding belief in the transformative power of education.

Eleanor's formative years were marked by a series of heart-wrenching losses. At the tender age of eight, she suffered the devastating blow of her mother's untimely death, leaving her bereft of maternal guidance. This profound loss would be compounded by the subsequent separation from her beloved father, who would succumb to the darkness of addiction.

Struggling through the tempest of these tragedies, young Eleanor found sanctuary in the halls of Allenswood, a prestigious boarding school in England. There, under the tutelage of formidable headmistress Marie Souvestre, she discovered a refuge from the tumultuous storms of her life. Souvestre, a beacon of intellectual enlightenment and progressive ideas, sparked in Eleanor a fervent desire for knowledge, instilling in her a firm belief in the inherent worth of every human being.

Returning to the shores of America, Eleanor's education continued to shape her worldview. She witnessed the stark contrast between the opulence of her privileged upbringing and the harsh realities faced by those less fortunate. This stark dichotomy would become a driving force, fueling her unwavering dedication to social justice and the pursuit of equality.

Marriage to Franklin D. Roosevelt

In the summer of 1902, Eleanor Roosevelt returned to her childhood home in Tivoli, New York and encountered Franklin Delano Roosevelt, her father's fifth cousin, on a train journey that would forever bind their lives together. Their courtship unfolded gradually over the following years, fueled by a steady exchange of letters and occasional meetings. Franklin, the charming suitor, courted Eleanor with a mixture of intellectual banter and earnest affection. Their letters, filled with youthful optimism and shared dreams, revealed the deepening bond between them.

On March 17, 1905, Eleanor and Franklin exchanged their vows in an intimate ceremony in New York City, embarking on a journey as husband and wife. Bound by a deep sense of mutual respect, love, and a shared vision for a better future, their union set the stage for a partnership that would profoundly shape the course of their lives and the destiny of a nation.

First Lady of New York

In the corridors of power, where the echoes of ambition reverberate and the wheels of progress grind, Eleanor Roosevelt emerged as a formidable force during her tenure as First Lady of New York. She embarked on a crusade that would forever transform the lives of countless New Yorkers, particularly the marginalized and forgotten.

As Eleanor assumed the mantle of First Lady of New York, she understood the weight of responsibility that rested upon her slender shoulders. She saw her new role not as a mere ceremonial position but as a platform from which she could effect tangible change, an opportunity to uplift the downtrodden and give voice to the voiceless.

Housing, a fundamental need often denied to the most vulnerable, became a focal point of Eleanor's efforts. She witnessed firsthand the dire living conditions faced by many New Yorkers, particularly those in impoverished neighborhoods. With a dogged determination, she advocated for the improvement of housing conditions, spearheading initiatives to address the dearth of affordable housing. Eleanor's vision of a more equitable society demanded that no individual be deprived of the basic dignity of a safe and decent home.

Education, a beacon of hope and opportunity, was another realm in which Eleanor sought to effect lasting change. Believing fervently in the transformative power of education, she championed initiatives to improve access to quality schooling for all children, regardless of their background or socioeconomic status. With her unyielding commitment to equal educational opportunities, she fought tirelessly to bridge the gap between privilege and poverty, recognizing that education was the key that unlocked the doors of possibility for generations to come.

Yet, Eleanor's endeavors went beyond mere policy initiatives. She understood the importance of personal connection, of engaging directly with the people whose lives she sought to improve. She immersed herself in the lives of ordinary New Yorkers, listening to their stories, their hopes, and their dreams. Whether in tenement apartments or community centers, Eleanor's compassion and genuine interest in the well-being of others left an indelible mark on those she encountered. Her commitment to the principles of fairness and equality set the stage for her future accomplishments as First Lady of the United States.

First Lady of the United States

On March 4, 1933, Eleanor Roosevelt assumed the mantle of First Lady of the United States with a resolute determination to redefine the role, to transcend mere ornamentation and chart a new course for women in the corridors of influence. As the nation grappled with the ravages of the Great Depression, Eleanor emerged as a beacon of hope, wielding her position with conviction to champion the causes of civil rights and women's rights.

In an era when the voices of women were often muted, Eleanor refused to be silenced. She shattered the confines of traditional expectations, stepping into the public sphere as a force to be reckoned with.

Her advocacy for civil rights became a defining aspect of her tenure, propelling her into uncharted territory and setting her apart as a champion of the marginalized.

Eleanor's commitment to civil rights was rooted in her belief in the inherent worth and dignity of every human being. She stood at the forefront of the fight against racial discrimination, fearlessly challenging the prevailing norms of a society steeped in systemic prejudice. With courage and conviction, she lent her support to organizations dedicated to the advancement of African Americans, defying the critics and risking her own standing to ensure that the arc of justice bent ever closer to equality.

In a time when women's rights were relegated to the periphery, Eleanor emerged as a fierce advocate for gender equality. She recognized that true progress could only be achieved through the empowerment of women, and she fought tirelessly to dismantle the barriers that held them back. From her platform as First Lady, she worked to expand educational opportunities for women, promote their economic independence, and push for equal representation in political and social spheres. Her efforts laid the foundation for future generations of women who would stand on her shoulders and carry the torch of progress forward.

While her tireless advocacy often brought her into conflict with those who sought to maintain the status quo, Eleanor's indomitable spirit remained unyielding.

Her vision for a more just and inclusive society guided her every step, and she refused to compromise in the face of adversity.

As First Lady of the United States, Eleanor Roosevelt forged a new path, redefining the role and pushing the boundaries of possibility, ultimately leaving an indelible mark on the pages of American history.

World War II and the United Nations

As the dark clouds of World War II loomed over the horizon, Eleanor Roosevelt emerged as a towering figure of resilience and fortitude. Her commitment to justice and her efforts on the world stage would forever alter the course of history, guiding the United States through one of its most challenging eras and helping shape the formation of the United Nations.

She traveled to war-torn regions, witnessing the devastation firsthand and lending her voice to the plight of those affected by conflict. In doing so, she played a crucial role in shaping the nation's response to the atrocities committed during World War II.

It was during this tumultuous period that Eleanor Roosevelt's vision for a more just and peaceful world crystallized. She recognized that the global community needed an institution that would serve as a forum for nations to come together, to resolve conflicts through diplomacy and to uphold the principles of human rights.

Eleanor's belief in the power of international cooperation led her to play a pivotal role in the creation of the United Nations.

As the United Nations Charter took shape, Eleanor tirelessly lobbied for its inclusion of fundamental human rights. She played a crucial role in the drafting of the Universal Declaration of Human Rights, ensuring that the ideals of justice, equality, and freedom would form the bedrock of the United Nations' mission. Her tireless advocacy towards protection of human rights left an indelible mark on this historic document, shaping the way nations approach the protection of individual liberties to this day.

With the establishment of the United Nations, Eleanor Roosevelt found herself at the nexus of global affairs. She served as the United States delegate to the United Nations General Assembly, bringing her formidable intellect and unyielding dedication to the table. Her voice, filled with compassion and a resolute belief in the potential of humanity, became a beacon of hope in a world still reeling from the horrors of war.

Post-War Activism

The echoes of war may have faded, but the flames of Eleanor Roosevelt's activism continued to burn brightly in the post-war period. She embarked on a new chapter of her life, dedicating herself to the causes of refugees, human rights, and environmental conservation.

In the wake of the devastating conflict, Eleanor turned her attention to the plight of those displaced by war. She witnessed firsthand the suffering of refugees, their lives uprooted, their hopes shattered. With her characteristic empathy and a steadfast commitment to the most vulnerable among us, she became a tireless advocate for the rights and well-being of refugees.

Eleanor lent her voice and her influence to organizations dedicated to providing aid and resettlement for those who had lost everything. She championed the cause of refugees, reminding the world that compassion knows no borders and that our shared humanity demands that we extend a helping hand to those in need.

But Eleanor's activism extended far beyond the realm of refugees. She recognized that the fight for human rights remained an ongoing struggle, one that required vigilance and commitment. She spoke out against racial discrimination, segregation, and the continued denial of basic rights to marginalized communities. Her voice, resonant with the passion of a lifetime of advocacy, reverberated across the nation and beyond, inspiring generations to continue the fight for equality and justice.

In an era when environmental conservation was often overlooked, Eleanor Roosevelt stood as a fierce advocate for the protection of our planet. She recognized the interconnectedness of human welfare and the health of the natural world.

With her characteristic foresight and wisdom, she saw that a sustainable future demanded our stewardship of the earth and the preservation of its precious resources.

Eleanor lent her support to organizations and initiatives dedicated to environmental conservation, emphasizing the importance of responsible and sustainable practices. Her advocacy for the environment, ahead of its time, served as a clarion call to future generations, urging us to recognize our shared responsibility to safeguard the planet for future generations.

Personal Life

Beneath the veneer of Eleanor Roosevelt's public persona lay a woman grappling with personal struggles, a tapestry woven with threads of heartache, resilience, and the complexities of human relationships. Behind the scenes of her public life, Eleanor navigated the treacherous waters of her personal journey, facing challenges that tested her spirit and shaped the contours of her character.

One of the most formidable obstacles she encountered was her fraught relationship with her mother-in-law, Sara Delano Roosevelt. The clash between these two strong-willed women, both fiercely protective of their respective domains, was a source of tension throughout Eleanor's life. Sara, with her steely resolve and unyielding expectations, often overshadowed Eleanor, leaving her feeling confined and diminished.

Yet, within the confines of this challenging relationship, Eleanor found the inner strength to carve out her own path, establishing her own identity separate from the formidable shadow cast by her mother-in-law.

Complicating matters further was the painful knowledge of her husband Franklin D. Roosevelt's infidelity. Eleanor bore witness to the extramarital affairs that cast a long shadow over their marriage. The betrayal cut deep, testing the bonds of trust and challenging her resolve to maintain the façade of a perfect union. Despite the personal anguish she endured, Eleanor's commitment to her marriage and her sense of duty to her family propelled her forward, navigating the tumultuous waters of a complicated relationship with resilience and grace.

In the midst of these personal struggles, Eleanor sought solace and connection outside the confines of her marriage. Her own romantic relationships, most notably her deep emotional bond with Lorena Hickok, brought both joy and turbulence into her life. The complexities of their relationship, rooted in a shared passion for social justice and a deep emotional connection, presented Eleanor with an opportunity for personal growth and self-discovery.

Despite the personal trials she faced, Eleanor Roosevelt emerged as a pillar of strength, her resilience forged in the crucible of adversity.

She defied societal norms, challenging the boundaries of what was expected of a woman in her time. Eleanor's personal struggles, though often overshadowed by her public achievements, were an integral part of her journey, shaping her character and lending depth to her advocacy.

Legacy and Impact

Eleanor Roosevelt's legacy is etched deeply into the fabric of American politics and society. Her influence reached far beyond her time, resonating with generations to come and shaping the course of civil rights, women's rights, and human rights.

Eleanor's impact extended far beyond the borders of the United States. Her voice, amplified by her position on the world stage, resonated with people around the globe. She became a beacon of hope for the oppressed, a champion for the marginalized, and an inspiration for those yearning for a more just and inclusive world. Her example continues to guide activists, leaders, and ordinary citizens alike, reminding us that one person, driven by compassion and conviction, can make a profound difference in the world.

Eleanor Roosevelt's legacy is one of resilience, compassion, and unwavering dedication to the principles she held dear. Her impact on American politics and society remains a guiding force, reminding us of the power of advocacy, the importance of empathy, and the enduring quest for justice. Her life is a testament to the capacity of individuals to effect change, to rise above adversity, and to leave an indelible mark on the world.

It is a brave thing to
have courage to be an
individual; it is also,
perhaps, a lonely thing.
But it is better than not
being an individual,
which is to be
nobody at all.

Eleanor Roosevelt's
little book of
selected quotes

Each time you learn
something new you
must readjust the
whole framework of
your knowledge.

A little
simplification
would be the first
step toward rational
living, I think.

Eleanor Roosevelt's
little book of
selected quotes

There never has been security. No man has ever known what he would meet around the next corner; if life were predictable it would cease to be life, and be without flavor.

Eleanor Roosevelt's little book of selected quotes

Friendship with oneself
is all-important,
because without it
one cannot be friends
with anyone else
in the world.

Eleanor Roosevelt's
little book of
selected quotes

The more we simplify
our material needs
the more we are free
to think of other
things.

All wars eventually
act as boomerangs
and the victor
suffers as much as
the vanquished.

Eleanor Roosevelt's
little book of
selected quotes

I often wonder how
we can make the more
fortunate in this
country fully aware of
the fact that the problem
of the unemployed is not
a mechanical one. It is a
problem alive and
throbbing with
human pain.

Eleanor Roosevelt's
little book of
selected quotes

Success must
include two things:
the development of
an individual to his
utmost potentiality and
a contribution of some
kind to one's world.

Eleanor Roosevelt's
little book of
selected quotes

We all create the person we become by our choices as we go through life. In a real sense, by the time we are adults, we are the sum total of the choices we have made.

Eleanor Roosevelt's little book of selected quotes

True patriotism springs from a belief in the dignity of the individual, freedom and equality not only for Americans but for all people on earth, universal brotherhood and good will, and a constant and earnest striving toward the principles and ideals on which this country was founded.

Someone once asked me what I regarded as the three most important requirements for happiness. My answer was: A feeling that you have been honest with yourself and those around you; a feeling that you have done the best you could both in your personal life and in your work; and the ability to love others.

Eleanor Roosevelt's little book of selected quotes

I have spent many
years of my life in
opposition, and I
rather like the role.

Because they
have so little,
children must rely
on imagination
rather than
experience.

Eleanor Roosevelt's
little book of
selected quotes

Will people ever be wise enough to refuse to follow bad leaders or to take away the freedom of other people?

Eleanor Roosevelt's little book of selected quotes

Only a man's
character is the real
criterion of worth.

Conservation of land
and conservation of
people frequently go
hand in hand.

I cannot believe
that war is the
best solution.
No one won the last
war, and no one will
win the next war.

Eleanor Roosevelt's
little book of
selected quotes

I think the thing we must look for actually is a growth in our people and in whoever comes in a quality of courage to tell our people just what world conditions are.

Eleanor Roosevelt's little book of selected quotes

Everyone has the right
to rest and leisure,
including reasonable
limitation of working
hours and periodic
holidays with pay.

Eleanor Roosevelt's
little book of
selected quotes

I was one of those who was
very happy when the original
prohibition amendment passed.
I thought innocently that a
law in this country would
automatically be complied with,
and my own observation led me
to feel rather ardently that
the less strong liquor anyone
consumed the better it was.
During prohibition I observed
the law meticulously, but I came
gradually to see that laws are
only observed with the consent
of the individuals concerned
and a moral change still
depends on the individual and
not on the passage of any law.

Eleanor Roosevelt's
little book of
selected quotes

Freedom makes a
huge requirement of
every human being.
With freedom comes
responsibility.
For the person who is
unwilling to grow up,
the person who does
not want to carry is
own weight, this is a
frightening prospect.

Eleanor Roosevelt's
little book of
selected quotes

Ability is not
something to be saved,
like money, in the hope
that you can draw
interest on it. The
interest comes from
the spending. Unused
ability, like unused
muscles, will atrophy.

Eleanor Roosevelt's
little book of
selected quotes

Courage is more exhilarating than fear and in the long run it is easier. We do not have to become heroes over night. Just a step at a time, meeting each thing that comes up, seeing it is not as dreadful as it appeared, discovering we have the strength to stare it down.

Eleanor Roosevelt's little book of selected quotes

We need emotional
outlets in this country,
and the more artistic
people we develop the
better it will be for
us as a nation.

No man is defeated
without until he has
first been defeated
within.

Each generation
supposes that the
world was simpler
for the one before it.

Eleanor Roosevelt's
little book of
selected quotes

Life has got to be lived — that's all there is to it. At seventy, I would say the advantage is that you take life more calmly. You have that 'This, too, shall pass!'

We face the future fortified with the lessons we have learned from the past. It is today that we must create the world of the future. Spinoza, I think, pointed out that we ourselves can make experience valuable when, by imagination and reason, we turn it into foresight.

Eleanor Roosevelt's little book of selected quotes

Too many of us stay walled up because we are afraid of being hurt. We are afraid to care too much, for fear that the other person does not care at all.

Eleanor Roosevelt's little book of selected quotes

I found that
almost everyone
had something
interesting to
contribute to
my education.

More people
are ruined
by victory,
I imagine,
than by defeat.

Eleanor Roosevelt's
little book of
selected quotes

About the only value the story of my life may have is to show that one can, even without any particular gifts, overcome obstacles that seem insurmountable if one is willing to face the fact that they must be overcome.

No human being can
ever 'own' another,
whether in friendship,
love, marriage, or
parenthood.

Eleanor Roosevelt's
little book of
selected quotes

I say to the young: Do not stop thinking of life as an adventure. You have no security unless you can live bravely, excitingly, imaginatively.

Eleanor Roosevelt's little book of selected quotes

All of us in this country give lip service to the ideals set forth in the Bill of Rights and emphasized by every additional amendment, and yet when war is stirring in the world, many of us are ready to curtail our civil liberties. We do not stop to think that curtailing these liberties may in the end bring us a greater danger than the danger we are trying to avert.

Eleanor Roosevelt's little book of selected quotes

Happiness is not a goal,
it is a by-product.
Paradoxically, the one
sure way not to be happy
is deliberately to map
out a way of life in
which one would please
oneself completely
and exclusively.

Eleanor Roosevelt's
little book of
selected quotes

It isn't enough to talk about peace. One must believe in it. And it isn't enough to believe in it. One must work at it.

A democratic form
of government, a
democratic way of life,
presupposes free public
education over a long
period; it presupposes
also an education for
personal responsibility
that too often is
neglected.

Eleanor Roosevelt's
little book of
selected quotes

When you adopt the standards and the values of someone else ... you surrender your own integrity. You become, to the extent of your surrender, less of a human being.

Strength that goes
wrong is even more
dangerous than
weakness that
goes wrong.

One has to live in
Washington to know
what a city of
rumors it is.

Eleanor Roosevelt's
little book of
selected quotes

Surely, in the light of history, it is more intelligent to hope rather than to fear, to try rather than not to try. For one thing we know beyond all doubt: nothing has ever been achieved by the person who says: it can't be done.

Eleanor Roosevelt's little book of selected quotes

The greatest luxury
I know is sitting up
reading in bed.

The first freedom
of man, I contend,
is the freedom to eat.

The arts in every
field — music, drama,
sculpture, painting
— we can learn to
appreciate and enjoy.
We need not be
artists, but we
should be able to
appreciate the work
of artists.

Eleanor Roosevelt's
little book of
selected quotes

Hate and force cannot
be in just a part of
the world without
having an effect on
the rest of it.

Eleanor Roosevelt's
little book of
selected quotes

Sometimes I wonder if we shall ever grow up in our politics and say definite things which mean something, or whether we shall always go on using generalities to which everyone can subscribe, and which mean very little.

A mature person is one who does not think only in absolutes, who is able to be objective even when deeply stirred emotionally, who has learned that there is both good and bad in all people and all things, and who walks humbly and deals charitably with the circumstances of life, knowing that in this world no one is all-knowing and therefore all of us need both love and charity.

You get more joy
out of the giving to
others, and should
put a good deal of
thought into the
happiness you are
able to give.

Eleanor Roosevelt's
little book of
selected quotes

Long ago, I made up my mind that when things were said involving only me, I would pay no attention to them, except when valid criticism was carried by which I could profit.

Eleanor Roosevelt's little book of selected quotes

No one can make
you feel inferior
without your
consent.

It is not fair to
ask of others what
you are unwilling
to do yourself.

Eleanor Roosevelt's
little book of
selected quotes

We can no longer oversimplify. We can no longer build lazy and false stereotypes: Americans are like this, Russians are like that, a Jew behaves in such a way, a Negro thinks in a different way. The lazy generalities – 'You know how women are... Isn't that just like a man?' The world cannot be understood from a single point of view.

Eleanor Roosevelt's little book of selected quotes

What we must learn
to do is to create
unbreakable bonds
between the sciences
and the humanities.
We cannot
procrastinate.
The world
of the future
is in our making.
Tomorrow is now.

Eleanor Roosevelt's
little book of
selected quotes

The important thing
is neither your
nationality nor
the religion you
professed, but how
your faith translated
itself in your life.

Eleanor Roosevelt's
little book of
selected quotes

Up to a certain point it is good for us to know that there are people in the world who will give us love and unquestioned loyalty to the limit of their ability. I doubt, however, if it is good for us to feel assured of this without the accompanying obligation of having to justify this devotion by our behavior.

Eleanor Roosevelt's little book of selected quotes

You gain strength, courage and confidence by every experience in which you really stop to look fear in the face. You are able to say to yourself, "I have lived through this horror. I can take the next thing that comes along." ... You must do the thing you think you cannot do.

Eleanor Roosevelt's little book of selected quotes

The will of the people shall be the basis of the authority of government...

There are practical little things in housekeeping which no man really understands.

Eleanor Roosevelt's little book of selected quotes

The motivating force
of the theory of a
Democratic way of life
is still a belief that as
individuals we live
cooperatively, and, to
the best of our ability,
serve the community in
which we live...

Eleanor Roosevelt's
little book of
selected quotes

A consciousness of the fact that war means practically total destruction is the reason, I think, for the rising tide to prevent what seems such a senseless procedure.
I understand that it is perhaps difficult for some people, whose lives have been lived with a sense of the need for military development, to envisage the possibility of being no longer needed. But the average citizen is beginning to think more and more of the need to develop machinery to settle difficulties in the world without destruction or the use of atomic bombs.

The trouble is that not enough people have come together with the firm determination to live the things which they say they believe.

Where, after all, do universal human rights begin? In small places, close to home – so close and so small that they cannot be seen on any maps of the world... Such are the places where every man, woman and child seeks equal justice, equal opportunity, equal dignity without discrimination. Unless these rights have meaning there, they have little meaning anywhere.

Eleanor Roosevelt's little book of selected quotes

Nothing alive can stand still, it goes forward or back. Life is interesting only as long as it is a process of growth; or, to put it another way, we can only grow as long as we are interested.

Eleanor Roosevelt's little book of selected quotes

At all times, day
by day, we have to
continue fighting for
freedom of religion,
freedom of speech,
and freedom from want
— for these are
things that must be
gained in peace as
well as in war.

Eleanor Roosevelt's
little book of
selected quotes

Caring comes from
being able to put
yourself in the
position of the
other person.

You always admire
what you really
don't understand.

Eleanor Roosevelt's
little book of
selected quotes

I think, at a child's birth, if a mother could ask a fairy godmother to endow it with the most useful gift, that gift would be curiosity.

Eleanor Roosevelt's little book of selected quotes

If you can develop
this ability to see
what you look at,
to understand its
meaning, to readjust
your knowledge to
this new information,
you can continue to
learn and to grow as
long as you live
and you'll have a
wonderful time
doing it.

Eleanor Roosevelt's
little book of
selected quotes

When will our consciences grow so tender that we will act to prevent human misery rather than avenge it?

Eleanor Roosevelt's little book of selected quotes

I kept praying that
I might be able to
prevent a repetition
of this stupidity
called war. I have
tried to keep the
promise I made to
myself, but the
progress that the
world is making
toward peace seems
like the crawling of a
little child, very
halting and slow.

Eleanor Roosevelt's
little book of
selected quotes

The things you refuse
to meet today always
come back at you
later on, usually
under circumstances
which make the
decision twice as
difficult as it
originally was.

Eleanor Roosevelt's
little book of
selected quotes

As long as we are not actually destroyed, we can work to gain greater understanding of other peoples and to try to present to the peoples of the world the values of our own beliefs. We can do this by demonstrating our conviction that human life is worth preserving and that we are willing to help others to enjoy benefits of our civilization just as we have enjoyed it.

Eleanor Roosevelt's little book of selected quotes

We will never
have peace without
friendship around
the world.

Talking too much
is a far greater
social fault than
talking too little.

Too often the great
decisions are originated
and given form in bodies
made up wholly of men, or
so completely dominated
by them that whatever of
special value women have
to offer is shunted aside
without expression.

Eleanor Roosevelt's
little book of
selected quotes

Anyone who knows
history, particularly
the history of Europe,
will, I think, recognize
that the domination
of education or of
government by any one
particular religious
faith is never a happy
arrangement for
the people.

Eleanor Roosevelt's
little book of
selected quotes

A successful life for a man or for a woman seems to me to lie in the knowledge that one has developed to the limit the capacities with which one was endowed; that one has contributed something constructive to family and friends and to a home community; that one has brought happiness wherever it was possible; that one has earned one's way in the world, has kept some friends, and need not be ashamed to face oneself honestly.

Eleanor Roosevelt's little book of selected quotes

This [the arts] is an area where we have lagged far behind other countries. We have been so preoccupied with our industrial growth that we have thought of little else. The culture of a nation is, after all, as important as its economy.

To be mature you have to realize what you value most... Not to arrive at a clear understanding of one's own values is a tragic waste. You have missed the whole point of what life is for.

Eleanor Roosevelt's little book of selected quotes

It is curious how much more interest can be evoked by a mixture of gossip, romance, and mystery than by facts.

The greatest tragedy of old age is the tendency for the old to feel unneeded, unwanted, and of no use to anyone; the secret of happiness in the declining years is to remain interested in life, as active as possible, useful to others, busy, and forward looking.

Practically nothing we do ever stands by itself. If it is good, it will serve some good purpose in the future. If it is evil, it may haunt us and handicap our efforts in unimagined ways.

Eleanor Roosevelt's little book of selected quotes

I think we ought to impress on both our girls and boys that successful marriages require just as much work, just as much intelligence and just as much unselfish devotion, as they give to any position they undertake to fill on a paid basis.

Eleanor Roosevelt's little book of selected quotes

We are given in our
newspapers and on TV
and radio exactly what
we, the public, insist
on having, and this
very frequently is
mediocre information
and mediocre
entertainment.

Usefulness, whatever form it may take, is the price we should pay for the air we breathe and the food we eat and the privilege of being alive.

Eleanor Roosevelt's little book of selected quotes

Long ago, there was a noble word, liberal, which derives from the word free. Now a strange thing happened to that word. A man named Hitler made it a term of abuse, a matter of suspicion, because those who were not with him were against him, and liberals had no use for Hitler. And then another man named [Joseph] McCarthy cast the same opprobrium on the word.... We must cherish and honor the word free or it will cease to apply to us.

I believe in active citizenship, for men and women equally, as a simple matter of right and justice. I believe we will have better government in all of our countries when men and women discuss public issues together and make their decisions on the basis of their different areas of experience and their common concern for the welfare of their families and their world.

If the use of leisure time is confined to looking at TV for a few extra hours every day, we will deteriorate as a people.

Eleanor Roosevelt's little book of selected quotes

It is very difficult to have a free, fair and honest press anywhere in the world. In the first place, as a rule, papers are largely supported by advertising, and that immediately gives the advertisers a certain hold over the medium they use.

Eleanor Roosevelt's little book of selected quotes

If anyone were to ask me what I want out of life I would say- the opportunity for doing something useful, for in no other way, I am convinced, can true happiness be attained.

For all of us, as we grow older, perhaps the most important thing is to keep alive our love of others and to believe that our love and interest are as vitally necessary to them as to us. This is what makes us keep on growing and refills the fountains of energy.

Eleanor Roosevelt's little book of selected quotes

No matter how plain
a woman may be, if
truth and honesty
are written across
her face, she will
be beautiful.

There are three
fundamentals for
human happiness –
love and faith, and
work which will
produce at least a
minimum of material
security. These
things must be made
possible for all
human beings, men
and women alike.

Eleanor Roosevelt's
little book of
selected quotes

In times past, the
question usually asked
by women was "How can
we best help to defend
our nation?" I cannot
remember a time when
the question on so many
people's lips was "How
can we prevent war?"

Eleanor Roosevelt's
little book of
selected quotes

The most unhappy people in the world are those who face the days without knowing what to do with their time. But if you have more projects than you have time for, you are not going to be an unhappy person. This is as much a question of having imagination and curiosity as it is of actually making plans.

The only advantage of not being too good a housekeeper is that your guests are so pleased to feel how very much better they are.

Eleanor Roosevelt's little book of selected quotes

No, I have never
wanted to be a man.
I have often wanted
to be more effective
as a woman, but I
have never felt that
trousers would
do the trick!

Eleanor Roosevelt's
little book of
selected quotes

We should begin in our own environment and in our own community as far as possible to build a peace-loving attitude and learn to discipline ourselves to accept, in the small things of our lives, mediation and arbitration. As individuals, there is little that any of us can do to prevent an accidental use of bombs in the hands of those who already have them. We can register, however, with our government a firm protest against granting the knowledge and the use of these weapons to those who do not now have them.

One of the best ways
of enslaving a people
is to keep them
from education...
The second way of
enslaving a people is
to suppress the sources
of information, not
only by burning books
but by controlling all
the other ways in which
ideas are transmitted.

If man is to be liberated to enjoy more leisure, he must also be prepared to enjoy this leisure fully and creatively. For people to have more time to read, to take part in their civic obligations, to know more about how their government functions and who their officials are might mean in a democracy a great improvement in the democratic processes. Let's begin, then, to think how we can prepare old and young for these new opportunities. Let's not wait until they come upon us suddenly and we have a crisis that we will be ill prepared to meet.

Feelings, too, are facts. Emotion is a fact. Human experience is a fact. It is often possible to gain more real insight into human beings and their motivation by reading great fiction than by personal acquaintance.

Eleanor Roosevelt's little book of selected quotes

We have to face the fact that either all of us are going to die together or we are going to learn to live together and if we are to live together we have to talk.

Eleanor Roosevelt's little book of selected quotes

Curiously enough, it is often the people who refuse to assume any responsibility who are apt to be the sharpest critics of those who do.

Eleanor Roosevelt's little book of selected quotes

The fundamental right of freedom of thought and expression is essential. If you curtail what the other fellow says and does, you curtail what you yourself may say and do.

Eleanor Roosevelt's little book of selected quotes

It takes courage to love,
but pain through love
is the purifying fire
which those who love
generously know. We all
know people who are so
much afraid of pain that
they shut themselves up
like clams in a shell and,
giving out nothing,
receive nothing and
therefore shrink until
life is a mere living
death.

Eleanor Roosevelt's
little book of
selected quotes

Printed in Great Britain
by Amazon